God made me

Notes for parents and other adult readers

Sitting down to read a book with a young child is a special privilege, and helping them take early steps in getting to know their world, themselves and God is even more special. However this book is not just intended to be read, but to be a springboard for helping children learn throughout the day (Deuteronomy 6:4-7; Psalm 145:3-7). Here are a few tips to help you adapt your reading and help their learning go beyond these pages:

For really little ones: You don't need to read all the text on every page. Go slow with learning body parts: just hands at first (then feet). Point to the child's own body as you read (then they can point). As children learn new skills, refer to God (e.g. "Isn't God clever to give you hands that can clap? Thank you God!"). Learn numbers by saying "God gave you ears/legs/fingers/toes. Let's count them." (See the website for ideas for each page.)

For bigger ones: Help them think of other things they can do with their bodies and learn other body parts. Ask what they like to taste, smell etc. They can do actions for the rhyme. They could help you write their own action rhyme (e.g. "God made my hands and I can clap, God made my... and I can... God made all of me!"). Laugh together—can they make a funny face like the boy? (See the website for ideas for each page.)

Other Bible passages to look at: Genesis 1:26-27; Psalm 139:13.

Making books for/with your child: Photograph them doing things throughout the day (or older children can draw). Put the pictures in a book with captions (e.g. 'Thank you God that I can sing with my mouth.'). They can do craft with a caption on the finished craft (e.g. 'Look what I can do with my hands! Thank you God.')

Pray: Encourage your child to say (or you say) simple prayers thanking God that he made them and loves them.

For more details of these and other tips, see www.teachinglittleones.com/bflo.

GOD MADE ME © MATTHIAS MEDIA 2015

Matthias Media (St Matthias Press Ltd ACN 067 558 365) | Email: info@matthiasmedia.com.au
Internet: www.matthiasmedia.com | Please visit our website for current postal and telephone contact information.

All Scripture quotations in this publication are from the Good News Translation in Today's English Version - Second Edition Copyright © 1992 by American Bible Society. Used by permission.

ISBN 978 1 922206 85 5

Cover design and typesetting by Karen Tse.

Photos: See www.teachinglittleones.com/bflo/photocredits.html

I have two hands. God made my hands.

I can clap with my hands.
Thank you God that I can do lots of things
with my hands.

God made all my fingers too.
I have ten fingers!

I have two feet and God made them.

I have two arms and two legs.
God made them too.

God also made my elbows
and my knees and my ankles.

Thank you God for my hands, my feet, my arms,
my legs, my elbows, my knees and my ankles!
I can use them to walk and jump and dance.

I also have two eyes, two ears,
one mouth and one nose. God made them too!

With my eyes I can see and with my ears I can hear.

With my mouth I can eat and talk.
And with my nose I can smell.

God made my eyes. God made my nose.
God made my fingers, my ankles and toes.
God made my knees and my elbows.
God made all of me!

God's book, the Bible, says God made all of me!
And he loves me too.

God made "every part of me".

Psalm 139 verse 13

Thank you God for making all of me!